DANCEHALL

Tim Stobierski's debut volume, *Dancehall*, captures the thrall of first real love in Sapphic poems that tumble with excitement and tumult. I rooted for the lovers, feeling as swept away as the speaker is: "Harvest me by the handful;/tear me out of the black earth." Stobierski's stunning imagery will have you enthralled again with the love poem and clinging with suspense while riding the affair's arc.

–Pegi Deitz Shea, two-time winner of the Connecticut Book Award and author of *The Weight of Kindling*

Tim Stobierski's collection, *Dancehall*, is in itself an ode to love, with all its passion and contradictions, gifting readers a wisdom we could only learn through a language like his, a skillful juxtaposition of love and loss, tenderness and lust.

Stobierski is a master of craft, a speaker who knows how to feel, who knows that love is a journey and a puzzle. His titles intrigue, his last lines transport the reader far beyond the initial moment. Each short poem is a tender vignette that smacks of the truth of human relationships, each one a moment to be felt, tasted, savored, cold and warmth juxtaposed. In them, we feel the passion and contradictions, something between the tender and the tumultuous—something like love.

Tim Stobierski's poems speak to everyone. *Dancehall* is a welcome reminder of poetry's often overlooked power to awaken us to the beauty, complexity, and fragility of love, life, and the small gifts we often ignore.

–Pat Mottola, author of *After Hours*

This book works like the metal teeth of a zipper, alternating exigent heartbreak with love throes. You can read it in one sitting, persisting even as its teeth catch on and scrape your skin, because it is such a pleasure "to remember what it is like / to be so lonely."

–Darcie Dennigan, author of *Corinna A-Maying the Apocalypse* and *Madame X*

In these tender poems, Tim Stobierski traces the familiar yet always-wrenching arc of early love gained, then lost. And while the darlings here are queer and kissing in parking lots, this tale brings us right back to Dante's *Vita Nuova* and the love lyric's difficult task: to explore the particularities of a singular vanished beloved in language that allows its readers, its voyeurs, to feel intimately present."

–V. Penelope Pelizzon, author of *Whose Flesh Is Flame, Whose Bone Is Time*

In *Dancehall*, a love story in five acts, Stobierski selects, dissects, and presents a series of moments—ranging from the mundane to the passionate to the anguished—that, when strung together, tell the complicated story of loving someone fully. While each poem is strong on its own, the work is tied together by recurring themes, comparisons, and language that take the reader on a rollercoaster of love and loss. Both playful and hard-hitting, it's unputdownable.

–Catherine Cote, founder of Project Empathy

At first glance, *Dancehall* is a title that conjures, to some, Jamaican dancehall music and the various popular dances this reggae style and vibe created. But a dancehall is also a public hall or building in which people dance, whether you call it a club, a disco, or a nightspot.

Tim Stobierski's *Dancehall* is the tale of a queer love story enacted nimbly as image/word dances and flourishes on the page. The speaker in these poems invites the reader to consider the myriad ways narratives are crafted in poetic form. One is struck by the brevity Stobierski establishes with poems such as "Apolloniad," which calls upon Greek mythology, and one poem "Falling in love with you" that appears pirouette-like in all five "acts" of the collection. There is a lot to admire in Stobierski's collection of poems, and it's a gem I'll enjoy reading again and again.

–Sean Frederick Forbes, author of *Providencia*: a book of poems

Tim Stobierski's *Dancehall* traces romantic love from its early, ingenuous encounters, when one lover can entreat the other to "speak me into being" and the whole natural world — from the keenest flower to the ocean itself — grows more vital and fine. But Stobierski's book, like love itself, also embraces darkness. It goes on to explore that same love lost, as the speaker learns to "give praise to the shadow" in a renewed and more reflective effort to entwine the self and the other. These poems are acutely attuned to love's shadow and love's light.

–David Groff, author of *Live in Suspense*

Tim Stobierski is also the author of a prior work entitled *Chronicles of a Bee Whisperer.*

DANCEHALL

poems

Tim Stobierski

Antrim House
Bloomfield, Connecticut

Library of Congress Control Number: 2023903145

ISBN: 979-8-9865522-6-2

First Edition, 2023

Printed & bound by Ingram Content Group

Book design by Rennie McQuilkin

Front cover photo by Ed Freeman via Getty Images

On p.36, the lines *I thought I was over you / but then I dreamt we
were at Whole Foods / buying oranges* were inspired by the title of a
Spotify playlist uploaded by user "Bolt." On p.54, the phrase *give
praise to the shadows* was inspired by the title of Junichiro Tanizaki's
book on Japanese architecture and aesthetics, *In Praise of Shadows*.

Antrim House
860.217.0023
AntrimHouseBooks@gmail.com
www.AntrimHouseBooks.com
400 Seabury Dr., #5196, Bloomfield, CT 06002

For you, soft heart

ACKNOWLEDGMENTS

I would like to start by thanking my family and friends, who have always supported my writing and shown me love.

Rennie, thank you for seeing promise in this collection and working to get it into book-ready shape.

Gina, thank you for encouraging me to pause (a very valuable skill) and for encouraging me to take a risk (an even more valuable skill) and for simply being there to talk.

I'd like to thank the teachers whose lessons still guide me as I write: Sharon Bryan, for teaching me the importance of clarity; Penelope Pelizzon, for teaching me the importance of pushing an idea to its limits, even if it means cutting it back in the end; Darcie Dennigan, for teaching me that really, at the end of the day, there are no rules.

To Pegi, Pat, Sean, David, and Catherine—thank you for reading the collection and for writing such kind words.

To Margaret—thank you for your careful reading, your correspondence, and your generous recommendations, some of which made it into the book.

To my earliest readers—Sitara, Katie, Jensine, Kim, Kelly, Alyssa, Jake, Diane, Nanette—thank you for humoring my 2 a.m. texts and screenshots and emails and works-in-progress. A special thanks to Sitara, who on more than one occasion helped me choose between two versions of the same poem or line or stanza that differed by only a word.

And, of course, to all of those loves, however real or imagined, however long or short, that inspired such strong emotions and, in turn, these poems—thank you.

TABLE OF CONTENTS

DANCEHALL

ACT ONE

There was before, and then there was you.

There are days I question the sun—

early mornings, late March,
still chilled
by last night's frost;
the front yard maple
yet to unfurl its arms
and shake off that winter sleep;
one lone bird (a wren, perhaps?)
somewhere in the brush
crying out his lover's song;
and you, low over the hills,
red and ripe and
ready to become.

Just as sparrows

in an eclipse
will descend from the sky
and land in the brush,
unsure if it is dusk or dawn,
the first time I saw you
my heart fell at your feet.

You scooped it in your hands
and cleared away
the strands of grass
it had collected on the ground—
and though you could have kept it
for an eternity or more,
you held it for just a moment
before uncupping your hands
so it could resume its flight.

Apolloniad

He smells like cut grass
and gasoline
when he arrives
for your date.
His skin, touched by the sun,
glows from the meadow,
and you forget that he is an hour late.

You sip iced tea while he
gulps down his third glass of water,
as though it would evaporate
the second he looks away.
He's telling a joke
about some poor boy falling from the sky,
forgets the punch line,
and you can see that he's blushing.

When was the last time
someone made you smile like this—
as though the skies
could open in his eyes
with the intensity of the sun
and you would think nothing
of withering in his gaze?

Blink once, blink twice at the brilliance,
but do not look away,
lest you miss your chance to become cinders.

And like a word

I ache to be spoken—
to cling to your lip
and fall from your tongue—

to crack in your voice
and catch in your throat.

Speak me into being.

Falling in love with you

~9~

was like venturing into the sun
after spending hours in the darkroom.

These cold nights

breed the warmest moments:
Each of us, two tequilas deep—
your hands, under my shirt,
flat against my chest—
mine, clasped tight
around the small of your back,
pulling you closer—
snow and sleet catching,
melting in your hair.

Melody

That first April night you and I kissed
in the parking lot behind the bar,
I remember the rain
played piano on my skin—
soft and cool, a song
I'd known the lyrics to
so many years before,
sitting in the backseat of my mother's Volvo
as she drove me home from Sunday school
the week we had learned about grace.

The words escape me,
but with your lips against mine
I can almost hear the tune.

Frogsong

Frogsong, and you
sleeping in the bed beside me,
your breathing punctuated
by the soft ticking of a clock
and the sound of creaking floor beams
settling in the night.
Somewhere in the hills,
a low rumble of thunder—
you turn, and I find you in the crook of my arm.

When you wake

kiss me once
on the lips
in my sleep
before you go
so that when
I wake I
can write love
poems about you
the way your
lips feel in
my sleep

Blot

I would not care
if you took your thumb
and one by one
blotted out the stars—
wiped them clear from the sky—
so long as you held me
in the resulting darkness.

Scarborough unfolds

its grass-lined shore
through breaking waves
southwest
toward Old Orchard
and beyond.

The setting sun
drips slowly
toward the sea,
molten copper speck
pleading to be quenched.

I have walked this beach.
I have watched this sun.
I have felt this pleading.
But you, here, now—
this is new.

Ours was not love at first sight

It was a moonless August night—

stars and stars and stars
in their relentless swirl.

One sudden flashing streak.
Stars.

A second, brighter, longer.
Stars.

A peripheral third—barely there at all.
Stars.

Then all at once,
that Perseid rush.

ACT TWO

What I remember most of that night
is your breath, hot against my neck.

Appetite

Skin hungers for skin.
Much as any starving beast
seeks meat, then finds it,
I indulge in your soft touch,
lap the grease from your fingers.

Want

~*20*~

Press into me
as night
presses
into a canyon.

If tasting you is a sin

I'll damn myself
with the salt
of your thigh
on my tongue,
your alkalinity
on my lips.

Dancehall

The Lord, he dances on my tongue
in rhinestone tap shoes,
his footfalls keeping beat
alongside my heart—
when my tongue grazes
the space between your lips.

He sings backup in my fingertips,
thick cellist's notes
so crucial to the composition,
his voice a perfumed smoke—
when my fingertips land
on the soft of your thighs.

He shakes a tambourine beneath my skin,
an old dancehall tune
my father learned from his sister's boyfriend
one sticky summer in Harlem—
when my skin has had its fill
and aches for calm.

Dance Lord, sing Lord, shake
Lord, and at last be still.

Falling in love with you

was like hearing an old favorite song on the radio
and tripping over my tongue to remember the words.

Some nights, when you are mine

~24~

I want to carve my name in your skin
with my tongue—deep strokes
across your back and down your spine—
shape you into a monument.

And on those nights that I am yours,
my back likewise aches for your name.

There are rocks in Narragansett

that know your body
nearly as well as I do—
heavy black stones slick with sea moss
that have cushioned your backside
as I tasted the ocean salt
on your lips, your neck, your chest,
the ridge of your waistband—
pebbles and sea glass and sand
that have felt your toes
curl tight, tight, tight
and then release.

When I spread myself open

~26~

I find I am an ocean,
vast and dark and warm—
a southern sea—
and like the sea I come in waves:
first crest, then trough,
then crest, then trough,
then crest, then
breaking, breaking, breaking.

Do not temper me in oil

as cumin, chili, mustard—
I will not dance,
I will not sing,
I will not unfurl
my essence to you
in just the right heat.
I am already unfurled,
unfurling—
my hips splayed,
my back arched
over the white
formica countertop,
your hand between my legs.

The night of our first big fight

maybe an hour after the last
insult was thrown,
I watched you in the kitchen
as you peeled an orange—
dug your fingernails in
just deep enough to pierce the skin
without puncturing fruit,
used your thumbs to coax apart
the segments at their seams—
and even though
you had been inside me
not even 48 hours before,
it wasn't until then that I realized
just how gentle you could be.

You were still angry,
but when you walked by
you paused long enough
to hand me a wedge
and kiss me on my cheek.

When I say "fuck me"

~29~

I do not want you
to be gentle.
I do not want you
to make love.
I do not want you
to whisper poetry,
kiss me deeply.

I want you to fuck me.

There will be other nights
for those things.

Crease

~30~

If I am too much to hold,
fold me in half
so I will fit in your arms.

I've been creased before;
it doesn't hurt, I promise,
nearly as much as you would think.

ACT THREE

Wind and rain and clouds—but worse, still, the silence.

If this is it

~*~

rest your head upon my chest
one last time,
and I will run my fingers
through the soft hairs
at the nape of your neck.
If I feel the full weight of your head
press down toward my heart,
I will let you sleep.
If I feel your tears
pool against my skin,
I won't say a word.

Love does not grow on trees

all sickly sweet,
as plums
which, left on the bough
through a mild September,
fall and mash
and beckon wasps
approaching winter's frenzy.

Love does not grow out of the ground
all green and lush,
as grass
which, left to its own whims,
bolts and blooms
and goes to seed,
then withers—
poor thing.

Love grows where it can,
as mold
which accepts
a forgotten heel of bread
as food and home
and thrives
until discovered,
and thrown away.

Heartbreak echoes

There is, of course, that first momentous rip—
clear and fibrous and sharp
and so unlike any other pain you have ever felt.
Don't worry. It will heal.

It is the echoes that will get you,
dull and muffled as they are—
three months after bounding around that cavity in your chest,
hitting you as you stand in the grocery store checkout
and swear to God that's him the next queue over,
just a little bit shorter than you remember, and with greasier hair;
six months after, when you tell yourself you're ready
to go out on a date and you spend the night laughing, smiling,
and you lean in for that first kiss and smell a familiar cologne
and never call him again;
two years after, when you are finally at peace
and you hear through mutual friends that
he's engaged, and she's pregnant, and
you're fine—*no, no*—you're fine.

I thought I was over you

but then I dreamt we were at Whole Foods
buying oranges
two weeks before Christmas,
your stubborn, ungloved hand in mine
inside my jacket pocket
as we waited in line to pay
behind a woman and her son
and bounced our feet to the tune
when *Frosty the Snowman*
began to play over the intercom.

When I woke up
I had to fight the urge
to turn over and check your pillow.

Just as breathing

is hard while running a mile,
so, too, is learning to live without you.

So many moments each day
once filled with your presence—
the way you sipped your tea
and chewed your toast;
the way your cologne
lingered in the hall
hours after you'd leave for work;
the way I'd find
little hairs on the bathroom sink
for days after you would shave;
the weight of your body
pressing down on my chest
as I was brought to come—
are now filled just with me.

But just as breathing
slows once more, and calms
once the running stops,
so, too, does this get easier.

Falling in love with you

~38~

was like stepping out onto a frozen lake
and trusting that it would not crack.

And if you were to bare your teeth

~39~

I would bare my neck,
content
to feel your lips
upon my skin
once again, however brief,
however chapped,
however deep
the resulting cut.

I promise, I'll believe you

~40~

Just tell me those lies
you used to tell me
when I still loved you.

I do not want this heart

I do not want this heart—
it has grown teeth.
It chews right through itself
and spits up blood.

I do not want this heart,
so full of holes
it has forgotten how
to quicken, beat.

I do not want this heart—
this raging, feeble heart.
I do not want this heart.
I do not want this heart.

And yet, this heart is mine.
Damned heart, to still be mine.

Will your name cease

one day, to catch
in my throat?

Will old pictures,
one day, no longer
cast sand in my eye?

Maybe.
Maybe.

Some days when I'm still mad at you

I go down to the store
and pick up a bag
of Granny Smith apples,
use the self-checkout,
and pay for six pieces of fruit
when I know damn well
there are eight in the bag.

Auto da fé

You always liked those movies
where the romantic lead
would lose the girl
due to incompetence
or pride or lies,
but win her back
with some grand
declaration of love—
John Cusack
and his boombox,
Ryan Gosling in the rain—
penance,
then the promised forgiveness.

You offered me
no such auto da fé,
just three words
on a little white screen—
I miss you—
6 a.m. one Sunday morning.

ACT FOUR

And then at long last, the flowers sprang from my heart.

And if I am a spool of thread

sitting on a shelf inside your heart,
take me down, some days,
and run me through your fingertips.
Unroll me across the floor
until I am vast and open.
Trim my worn ends
and knot me into a doll.
Wring my neck.
Push your face
into my fraying chest
and cry fat, heavy tears.
I will catch them
and I will hold them
and, even if my color runs,
I will be glad you gave them to me.

Like the sands of Hammonasset

~48~

move beneath the sea—
pushed and tugged and
swirled by the ocean swell—
so too do I find my heart
caught in the eddies of your love.

Thirst

~49~

Your love gripped me
the way thirst grips a throat—
at first, imperceptible;
then, a notion;
then, a scratch; then
all at once
an urgency
to drink, or die.

Bounty

And when I feel your palm
expansive on my thigh,
I become sweetgrass.

Harvest me by the handful;
tear me out of the black earth.
I am yours, as much as you can hold.

Drag

~51~

If I am a canvas,
blank and taut,
drag your body
across my face
and make art.

Failed Haiku

~52~

My love for you
is as easy as the grass
which simply knows to grow.

Falling in love with you

~53~

was like baking a cake from scratch
with a recipe, but no measuring cups.

Praise

My favorite part of making love is after,
when you walk naked around the room
extinguishing the candles
that just moments before
had danced alongside us.

I watch, and give praise to the shadows
that lick your back, wrap around you
so fully, closer and closer
as each wick gives up its light
until all that is left is darkness
and your arms wrapped around me.

Prayer to Zao Shen, Stove-top God

Do not recount
the long-simmered porridge
that so thirsted for water
it became paste in the pot;

Do not recount
the too-hot curry
studded with so many chilies
it was like a shotgun to the tongue;

Do not recount
those poorly-pressed wontons
which spilled out their contents
for want of a tighter embrace;

Do not recount
those assassin's fishbones
which caught in our throats
like so many words—

Only my face, bathed
in rice steam mid-July,
so that when he comes home
he can eat.

And if I am a grain of rice

your heart, an empty pot,
I will take my place
beneath your lid
and accept
there will be others—
I cannot fill you, a grain, alone.
Nor can I become
without your walls,
your warmth, your
willingness
to transform.

"I love you"

can be so many things—
a dare, a threat, a plea—
a ready arrow that I've felt
drawn back and aimed at me.

But when I use those three words
they're a promise, a pledge, a prayer—
and in all my visions of the future,
I can't imagine you not there.

So I'll say it once: I love you.
I'll say it twice: I love you still.
I love you, I love you, I love you—
I always have, and I always will.

Kennebunkport

and fresh snow
and you three steps
ahead of me on the strand
and the black sky smudged
grapefruit and cantaloupe
with impending dawn
and two seagulls
at the water's lip
beseeching the sun
to quicken its rise
and a ring
in my jacket pocket
made warm with
three days
constant turning
and a wave
and a wave
and a wave
and a wave

ACT FIVE

It was always there, this preemptive, aching grief.

Windstorm

Night, and olive-black.
Our bedroom fan sits idle,
its steady whir replaced
by the cat's lowercase snore.
Occasionally, the house groans
like an old man stretching his legs.
The pipes rattle, the toilet runs.
I'm reminded of our first storm,
how we savored the squid-ink night.
We hadn't yet bought candles,
but managed to squeeze
just enough light
from each other's tongues
to reignite the sky.

Kintsugi

There are nights when I feel
tears shudder through me
searching for an escape—
however happy I am,
with you asleep beside me.

I'm sorry, those nights,
you got the me that has been broken.

But I am thankful, too,
that you helped me
pick the shards up off the ground
and sand down the sharpest edges;
held them in place
so that I could fill the cracks
with good strong lacquer,
dust them with powdered gold
to look like those deep mountain veins.

There are chips, still, and holes,
but when you hold me in your hands
and press your fingertips into the gaps,
it's easy to forget they're there.

Just as grey skies at Ogunquit

could not diminish the vast
Atlantic Ocean, one moment
could not diminish my love for you.

The waves carry on their undulations,
no matter the color of the sky.

Falling in love with you

~64~

was like finding the second half of a simile
and knowing the poem was done.

Cake

And on nights like tonight
when we're lying in bed
sharing the last slice of cake
from your birthday two nights ago,
and you smear my lip
with a fingertip's fill
of blue buttercream frosting,
lean in,
kiss it away,
I remember what it is like
to be so lonely.

Who will teach the boys to dance

when you are gone
and it's just me
and my big clumsy feet,
searching for a rhythm
long since buried with you?

I can sway them now,
tiny as they are—
one in each arm—
the way I swayed
during our first dance
four years ago
in that old reception hall,
but some nights they cry for you
and I don't know the moves
they ache for.

If I put away my grassy boots,
my steps will be lighter
and my pivots more fluid
and, though I know it won't be the same,
maybe it can be enough.

And as the cicada

which, born in dirt,
must shed its skin
before birthright wings
may unfurl, inflate
to carry it aloft in song—

when your shell no longer serves you,
cast it off.

Catching

How quickly we slip
from *are* to *were*, *am* to *was*—
like the grasses of the Carrizo,
which prove so lush
in the April bloom,
catching flame in the August sun,
we are one moment supple;
the next, husk;
the next, light.

There is a photo I keep

in a drawer in my desk
beneath the year's receipts and W-2s—
a hazy polaroid of us
in our old apartment in New Haven,
snapped after a night
of charcuterie, cards, and drinks.
We were mid-laugh.
I do not hide it away
to ward off tears, or keep at bay
sweet could-have-beens.
I hide it so that months from now
when I am filing my taxes
and scrambling to gather my forms,
I'll see us blurred, and young, and happy.

Like an hallelujah in an empty church

you echoed through me—

knocked the dust from my rafters
and filled me with song

that grew more joyous
the less discernible it became,

word turned cry turned
crescendo

turned redemptive hum,
then silence

silence
silence

I'll wait for you

~71~

the way fireflies wait for the rain—
low in the tall July grass,
wings heavy with humidity,
until the storm comes, passes,
and they can take their flight.

Do not wipe away my tears.

Let them gather and well as they will
until they overflow their banks
and barrel down toward my heart—
soft heart, warm heart
so willing to be broken.

ABOUT THE AUTHOR

Tim Stobierski writes about relationships. His work explores universal themes of love, lust, longing, and loss — presented through the lens of his own experiences as a queer man. His poetry has been published in a number of journals, including the *Connecticut River Review, Midwest Quarterly,* and *Grey Sparrow.* His first book of poetry, *Chronicles of a Bee Whisperer,* was published by River Otter Press in 2012.

To pay the bills, he is a freelance writer and content strategist focused on the world of finance, investing, fintech, insurance, and software. In his professional writing, he prides himself on his ability to help the reader understand complicated subjects easily, a quality that informs his poetry.

He is also the founder and editor of StudentDebtWarriors. com, a free resource for college students, graduates, and parents who are struggling to make sense of the complex world of student loans.

This book is set in Garamond Premier Pro, which was conceived in 1988 when type-designer Robert Slimbach visited the Plantin-Moretus Museum in Antwerp, Belgium, to study its collection of Claude Garamond's metal punches and typefaces. During the 1500s Garamond—a Parisian punch-cutter—produced a refined array of book types that combined an unprecedented degree of balance and elegance, for centuries standing as the pinnacle of beauty and practicality in type-founding. They were based on the handwriting of Angelo Vergecio, court librarian of the French king, Francis I. Slimbach has created a new interpretation based on Garamond's designs and on compatible italics cut by Robert Granjon, Garamond's contemporary.

Copies of this book are available
at all bookstores including Amazon
and can be ordered directly
from Tim Stobierski
(timothy.stobierski@gmail.com),
Send $18 per book
plus $4 shipping
by check payable
to Tim Stobierski.

•

For more information on the work of Tim Stobierski,
visit www.antrimhousebooks.com/authors.html

www.ingramcontent.com/pod-product-compliance
Lightning Source LLC
Chambersburg PA
CBHW021122130726
47988CB00003B/1128